Sweatshirts
With a
Twist™
edited by Julie Johnson

Table of Contents

FUCHSIA FUN JACKET
page 8

E-mail: Customer_Service@DRGnetwork.com

HOUSE of WHITE BIRCHES
PUBLISHERS SINCE 1947

Sweatshirts With a Twist is published by DRG, 306 East Parr Road, Berne, IN 46711, telephone (260) 589-4000. Printed in USA. Copyright © 2008 DRG. All rights reserved. This publication may not be reproduced in part or in whole without written permission from the publisher.

RETAIL STORES: If you would like to carry this pattern book or any other DRG publications, call the Wholesale Department at Annie's Attic to set up a direct account: (903) 636-4303. Also, request a complete listing of publications available from DRG.

Every effort has been made to ensure that the instructions in this pattern book are complete and accurate. We cannot, however, take responsibility for human error, typographical mistakes or variations in individual work.

ISBN: 978-1-59217-222-1
1 2 3 4 5 6 7 8 9

STAFF
Editor: Julie Johnson
Managing Editor: Dianne Schmidt
Technical Artist: Nicole Gage
Technical Editor: Marla Freeman
Copy Supervisor: Michelle Beck
Copy Editors: Nicki Lehman,
  Mary O'Donnell

Graphic Arts Supervisor: Ronda Bechinski
Graphic Artists: Erin Augsburger,
  Joanne Gonzalez
Art Director: Brad Snow
Assistant Art Director: Nick Pierce
Photography Supervisor: Tammy Christian
Photography: Matthew Owen
Photo Stylist: Tammy Steiner

Wearable Art

I'll never forget the evening when the husband of a close friend presented a monologue that we've christened *Ode to a Radish*. "The simple, humble radish," he lamented, "left to languish alone on the relish tray." "But why?" he cried. "It's brilliant red on the outside with a crisp, clean white interior, slightly hot, always crunchy and fresh, and nothing is more lip-smacking good than a radish, butter and white-bread sandwich."

Elaborate on his speech and apply it to a sweatshirt; and what he said does make sense.

A sweatshirt is easy to find, relatively inexpensive, simple to wash and wear, and in the past, worn just for tasks involving physical activity: lawn mowing, window scrubbing and football games. But it's so easy to transform this simple, humble ready-to-wear garment by adding designer spice—trims, appliqués, fabric paint, interesting fabric, buttons and quilting—to change it into wearable art.

So why not expand your realm of self-expression and create a unique piece of wearable art by starting with a sweatshirt. It really is easy to do so, provided you have the right tools, techniques and tips.

And to think, the inspiration for these wearable-art sweatshirt designs came from turning a lowly radish into something "lip-smacking good"!

Julie

Julie Johnson, editor

SWING ON BY
page 34

SOPHISTICATED SWIRLS
page 38

GROMMET ACCENTS
page 41

Sweatshirt Basics

By following these tips and techniques, you can turn an ordinary sweatshirt into a unique wearable in no time.

GENERAL INSTRUCTIONS

Selecting the Perfect Sweatshirt

Before shopping for your sweatshirt, look at the design elements and answer the following questions to determine the size needed: Will I be removing the banding on the sleeves or torso (requiring a larger size for longer sleeves)? Is the sweatshirt redesign a tailored look (requiring a fitted sweatshirt)? Is the design a jacket style or can I wear the redesign with no additional top underneath?

Though it's hard to anticipate shrinkage, try the sweatshirt on and check for sleeve length, body length and width before you purchase. Look at the shoulder-seam placement and the fullness around the bust, rib cage, waist and hips. As a standard rule of thumb, for a fitted style, you'll want a minimum of 3 inches of ease around your bust and waist, and 4 inches around your hips. For a jacket style, plan to increase these measurements a minimum of 3 inches.

The fit of a sweatshirt and the redesign will help determine whether to buy the sweatshirt in your size or go up a size. Remember, you'll be washing the sweatshirt (expect some shrinkage) and doing some manipulation to the seam allowance(s), so it's best to start on the generous side and remove excess fabric as you sew.

Getting Started

Prewash your sweatshirt, the coordinating fabrics and specialty trims. Because you're combining different fabric types, you'll want to remove shrinkage before you sew to avoid the surprises of different design elements shrinking differently.

Though it's fine to put your sweatshirt into the dryer, do not use fabric softener. The fabric softener leaves behind a residue that may not agree with all of the fusibles used for the design. Plus, softener may leave spots on some blended fabrics—not a great way to start your redesign!

Most trims can be hand-washed and line-dried.

The Pressing Matters

Lightly press your sweatshirt before sewing using a medium heat setting. If the ironing board's pad and cover is worn, insert a towel or scrap wool under the board cover. This will add extra padding so you don't press the knit fabric of the sweatshirt flat. Press trims and trim fabrics flat.

Try a Teflon press cloth for pressing knits. I invested in a Teflon press cloth large enough to cover any appliqué work. The press cloth can be used for pressing serger seams by laying the sweatshirt on the ironing board with the serger seam flat, then placing the Teflon cloth on top of the seam and using the tip of the iron to compress the serged seam and reduce bulk.

 HOUSE OF WHITE BIRCHES, BERNE, INDIANA 46711   DRGNETWORK.COM

CUTTING INSTRUCTIONS

Sweatshirt Body

To determine the center front of the sweatshirt, with wrong sides facing, match shoulder seams at neck intersection. Next, pin side seams from the bottom rib to the beginning of the armsyce. *Note: If the sweatshirt does not have side seams, continue pinning from the shoulder point to the lower sleeve seam at the armsyce.*

Lay the sweatshirt flat; lightly pat and smooth sweatshirt toward the center to determine the center front. Mark the center front at neck and lower rib edges.

Turn the sweatshirt to the wrong side and match side seams. Slide a narrow mat between the sweatshirt front and back. Use a long ruler to connect markings and mark with marking pen or chalk. Stabilize the center front with Wash-A-Way Wonder tape positioned ¼ inch from the centerline. Use a long ruler and rotary cutter to open center front. Turn sweatshirt to the right side.

Ribbing

Prior to removing neck, waist and/or cuff ribbing, set sewing machine to a narrow zigzag. Use Wash-A-Away thread to sew ⅛ inch next to the ribbing to prevent raveling and to stabilize the cut edge of the fabric (Figure 1).

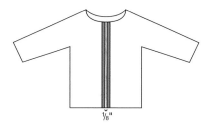

⅛"

Figure 1

Trim cuff ribbing using a 5-inch embroidery scissors to preserve as much sleeve length as possible. If sleeve length is not an issue, lightly press the sleeve flat using the sleeve seam as a guide. Place the sleeve on the cutting mat. Gently slide the ruler down toward the ribbing. Between the ruler and ribbing, use your rotary cutter to remove the ribbing.

SEWING MACHINE ADJUSTMENTS

Use polyester or a poly/cotton blend thread because polyester thread has more stretch to allow the seams to stretch with the knit fabric.

Use a ballpoint (stretch) needle. A ballpoint needle gently slips between the knit stitches and will not break the knit loops in the fabric. Also, this needle will leave smaller holes, making the topstitching more attractive.

Increase your stitch length to prevent the stitches from building up in the knit fabric and distorting the fabric as you sew. You may need to loosen the pressure on the presser foot if you notice the seam distorting (growing). Refer to your owner's manual if needed.

For weight-bearing seams (shoulder seams), zigzag over a piece of twill tape if desired. As you embellish the sweatshirt, more weight will be added to the body of the garment. The twill tape supports the weight of the fabric and prevents the shoulder seam from stretching as it's sewn and worn.

Instead of backstitching to secure threads, use seam sealant. Backstitching can cause the fabric at the beginning and end of each seam to distort. Try Fray Block, because the longer nozzle-tip gives better control when applying it in small amounts than other seam sealants.

SEWING ON BUTTONS

If a pattern calls for the addition of buttons as fasteners or trims, sew a smaller button on the back of the sweatshirt as you sew the main button on the outside. The inside button adds support so the outside button doesn't droop.

An alternative to a small button is to use a piece of binding or cotton fabric fused to the wrong side of the button placement.

INTERFACING TRICKS

Use knit or tricot lightweight interfacing for your sweatshirt redesign. Always use pinking shears to feather the edge of interfacing to prevent show-through of the interfacing on the front side of the sweatshirt.

Over time, the fusible bond of the knit interfacing may become loose due to the stretching of the knit fabric, so instead of fusing directly to the sweatshirt, shape lining from a lightweight woven and fuse the interfacing to the facing when feasible.

TO FACE OR NOT TO FACE

You may consider adding additional facing around the neck area. Most expensive T-shirts have a back facing to add support. To custom-cut one from your fabric, place the sweatshirt flat with the front open. Measure about 5 inches down the center back and draw a semicircular paper pattern to the shoulder seams, leaving a 1-inch width from the neck point (Figure 2).

Figure 2

Cut pattern from facing and edge-finish the raw edges of the back facing as desired. Lightly apply temporary spray adhesive to the wrong side of the facing and position along the neck seam. Topstitch into place.

SERGER SEAMING

A serger is a great way to eliminate bulk from seams. Instead of double-folding raw edges for hemming, use a 3- or 4-thread overlock on the serger to edge-finish and use your sewing machine to topstitch into place a single-fold hem.

If needed, serge over twill tape to support the weight of the sweatshirt and prevent distortion as described before.

Try using Stitch Witchery as you serge to help position facings. Lay the Stitch Witchery on the wrong side of the facing, and then serge facing and Stitch Witchery together as you edge-finish. Fold facing to the wrong side of the sweatshirt, press into place and topstitch as needed.

APPLIQUÉ TECHNIQUES

Apply fusible web to the back of the fabric to be appliquéd. Trace the design onto the paper backing of the appliqué fabric. Cut each shape from fabric with clean-cut lines. Trim any excess threads or uneven edges.

Stabilize the area on the wrong side of the sweatshirt with tricot interfacing by cutting the interfacing slightly larger than the appliqué with pinking shears. Fuse into place. Next, hand-baste or lightly apply temporary spray adhesive to adhere a mediumweight tear-away stabilizer beneath the sweatshirt area to be appliquéd.

Layer fabrics with sweatshirt right side up and position appliqué design as desired with right side up. Remove the paper backing from the appliqué. Place Teflon press cloth over appliqué and sweatshirt fabric. Use the tip of the iron to press appliqué piece to the sweatshirt, taking care to not distort the knit fabric.

Machine-baste into place. Attach an embroidery or zigzag foot and set the machine

for a satin stitch. Typically, the stitches should rest side by side, but use a slightly longer length to avoid the stitches building up on the fabric. Set your stitch width as desired. Loosen the needle tension to allow this thread to pull to the underside of the sweatshirt.

Satin-stitch appliqué into place. Remove tear-away stabilizer from the wrong side of the sweatshirt.

ADDING SIDE VENTS

Place Wash-A-Way Wonder tape on each side of a 3½-inch line starting at the bottom edge and continuing up the 3½-inch side (Figure 3) on the wrong side of the fabric. Position a small piece of tape across the top, contacting the two previous strips. Clip the line and snip into each corner to form a "Y" cut.

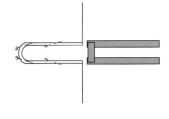

Figure 3

Cut an 18-inch length of bias tape. Cut in half to make two strips of tape. Press ¼ inch of the sweatshirt to the wrong side of the fabric covering the Wash-A-Way Wonder tape. Pin two lengths of the bias tape to cover the vertical raw edges of one vent. Add a small piece of the bias tape to cover the top raw edge. Use fabric glue and pins to hold in place (Figure 4).

Figure 4

Sewing from the wrong side (use your needle down position and a stiletto, if available), stitch into place. Repeat with a second row of stitches to secure edges of vent. Repeat for opposite side. ❖

Source: Wash-A-Way Wonder tape, Teflon appliqué press cloth, Wash-A-Way thread, stretch needles, Fray Block, 60-inch-wide Knit Fuse Interfacing, Sullivan's Quilt Basting Spray, Clover Bias Tape Makers, Clover Pen-Style Chaco Liners, Water-Erasable Blue Marking Pen, Iron Glide from Clotilde.com.

Fuchsia Fun Jacket

BY LONDA ROHLFING FOR LONDA'S CREATIVE THREADS

Stitch up a fun-inspired creation from Londa's Creative Threads.

FINISHED SIZE
Your size

MATERIALS
- Sweatshirt with dropped set-in sleeves
- Batik in multicolors featuring circles
- Iridescent dupioni
- Large decorative button
- Snap tape
- Lightly woven chenille yarn
- Woven fusible interfacing
- Fusible web tape
- Free-motion foot
- Darning needle
- Variegated heavy silk thread
- Basic sewing supplies and equipment

PROJECT NOTES
Designer's techniques have been developed for a high-quality, 80 percent cotton/20 percent polyester sweatshirt. Prewash sweatshirt.

Supplies and pattern for jacket are available at *Londa's Creative Threads/Londa's Creative Sweatshirt Jacket/Refined* at www.londas-sewing.com or www.makeasweatshirtjacket.com.

SWEATSHIRT PREPARATION
Note: *Enlarge front, back and sleeve templates (page 12) as indicated. Trace appropriate-size template pieces and cut out. Clip top slash mark on sleeve cap. Refer to General Instructions (page 4) throughout.*

1. Cut off the neckband, sleeve bands and lower band. Save the lower band to use as collar.

2. Press the sweatshirt flat to find the center side if no seams exist and slash up the side seams. If side seams do exist, remove seam from each side.

CUTTING SLEEVES
1. Cut off sleeves. Open along seam line.

2. Press pieces as flat as possible. **Note:** *Front and back will be left attached at shoulder seams for the time being.*

3. Position shaped sleeve template on sleeve approximately 2 inches down on side seam. Using rulers, extend the line of the sleeve template to the lower edge of the sleeve (Figure 1).

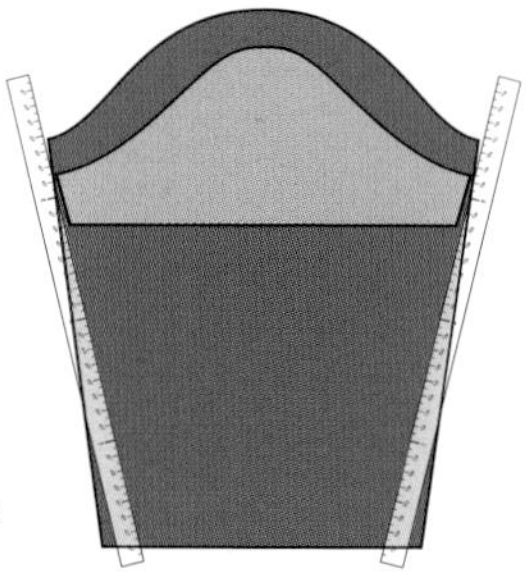

Figure 1

CUTTING FRONT & BACK
Note: *When recutting fronts and back, maintain as much body length and as much body width from the centers to the underarm as possible.*

1. Fold sweatshirt front and back in half, right sides together. Position front template on front fold (Figure 2) and cut out, extending line from underarm to lower edge of sweatshirt. **Note:** *Do not cut at neckline. You will be refining that in styling later.* Position back template on back fold and cut out in same manner.

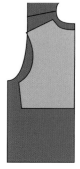

Figure 2

2. Remove templates and trim away uneven lines on armscyes if needed.

DESIGN & ASSEMBLY

Notes: *Back shoulder seams are designed longer and require easing of front pieces. Use ⅝-inch seam allowances unless otherwise stated. Trim and edge finish seams. Baste-fit before finishing seams or embellishing. The side of the jacket mentioned in instructions is stated as you are looking at the jacket.*

1. Find center front of sweatshirt; cut open. Fit to determine the angle and length of the front neckline. **Note:** *On model project, from shoulder to end of collar in front is 16¼ inches.* Press and cut off, allowing for a ¼-inch seam allowance (Figure 3). Flip cut-off piece, lay on top of opposite side and cut off identical amount (Figure 4). Staystitch neck edge.

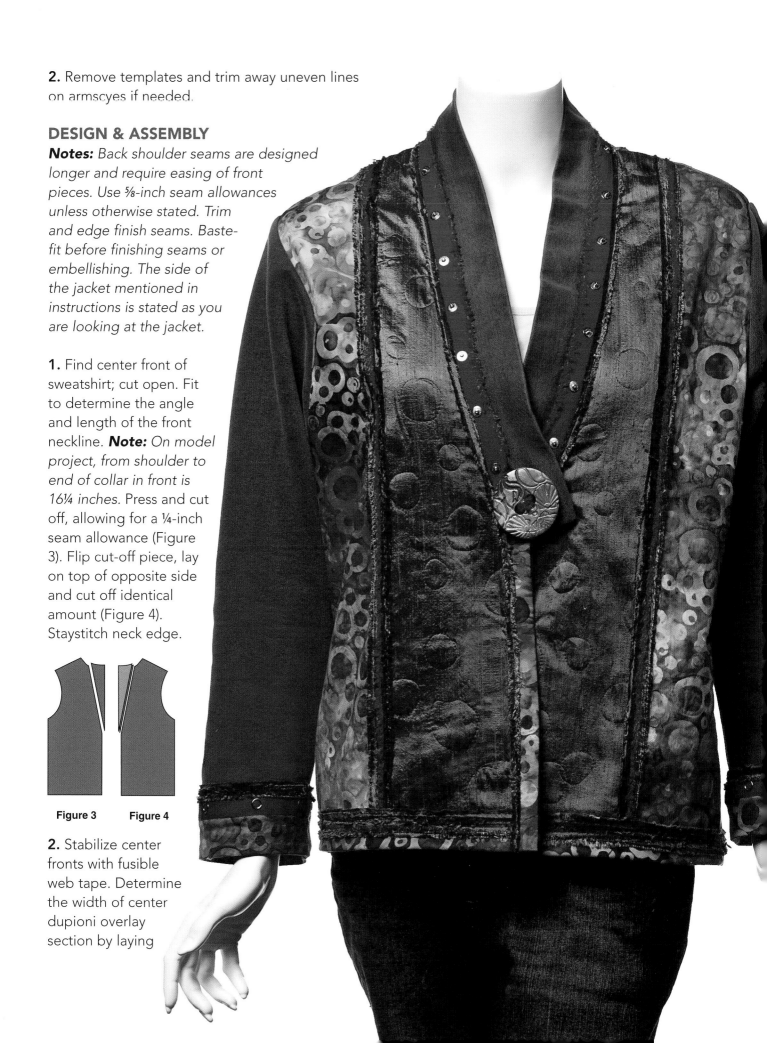

Figure 3   Figure 4

2. Stabilize center fronts with fusible web tape. Determine the width of center dupioni overlay section by laying the dupioni on the sweatshirt front. Sample overlay is slightly less than ½ of front panel. Cut slightly larger than needed (Figure 5). Pin in place.

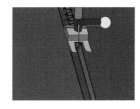

Figure 5

3. Using a free-motion foot, randomly stitch free-form circles over fabric to "quilt" the two pieces together and add texture. After quilting, straight-stitch along shoulders, center fronts and hem edges.

4. Cut remainder of fronts from batik fabric. Turn under long edges adjacent to the dupioni; stitch through both edges to attach to sweatshirt. Stitch around some of the circle motifs to quilt and add texture. Straight-stitch along shoulder, side and armscye edges.

5. Embellish the long joining seams by layering four ⅜- and ¼-inch strips of bias-cut dupioni stitched down the middle. Couch-stitch yarn over stitching (Figure 6).

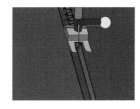

Figure 6

6. Repeat the process to cut a back yoke from dupioni, baste, quilt and embellish edges. **Note:** *At center back, yoke on model project measures 9 inches deep and extends into armscye 6½ inches from shoulder.*

7. Sew side seams in jacket. Sew sleeve seams; set in sleeves, easing to fit and matching seams. Stitch.

8. Check fit to determine hem length. Pin and press hem length. Trim on pressed line. Stabilize hem edge with fusible web tape. Cut a 2-inch-wide bias strip of batik fabric. Match right side of strip to wrong side of jacket hem. Sew strip to jacket using ¼-inch seam allowance. Press. Wrap strip to right side of jacket over hem edge and stitch ¾ inch from raw edge of strip. Over stitching, layer bias dupioni strips as follows: two ⅝-inch-wide strips, one ⅜-inch-wide strip, and two ¼-inch-wide strips. Stitch down the center through all layers.

9. For each sleeve cuff, cut a bias strip of batik fabric 5⅜ inches wide and long enough to fit around the end of the sleeve plus ½ inch. Interface with bias-cut woven interfacing 4⅜ inches wide. Sew short edges of each cuff together with right sides together using a ¼-inch seam allowance. Press. Slip cuff into sleeve with right side of cuff next to wrong side of sleeve. Sew around lower edge (Figure 7).

Figure 7

10. Pull cuff out and fold up over end of sleeve so length of cuff from inside seam to fold is 2¼ inches. Press. **Note:** *This allows the cuff to extend the length of the sleeve.* To embellish, cut and stitch a length of the female portion of snap tape along the upper edge of each cuff, stitching along each edge with a tiny zigzag stitch using monofilament thread. To finish, turn top edge under and overlap at beginning. On top edge of snap tape, layer bias-cut dupioni strips as outlined in step 8. Position so raw edge of cuff is exposed.

11. To finish center fronts, cut two 2⅝-inch strips of batik fabric the lengths of center fronts plus 2 inches. **Note:** *These can be straight or bias cut.* Stitch the right side of each strip to the wrong side of the jacket center front using a ⅜-inch seam, allowing strip to extend ½ inch or more at hemline. Trim seam allowance if needed. Press. At hem, trim excess to ½ inch; turn to inside and press. Wrap strip to right side of jacket. Stitch down along edge. Embellish using three ¼-inch bias strips of dupioni.

12. Trim seam allowance from lower band (ribbing) for collar. Measure jacket neckline from front opening to shoulder, around back to next shoulder and continue to opposite front opening. Add 1¼ inches to this measurement. Use this measurement to cut collar from lower band. **Note:** *Collar should be long enough to overlap the center front bias trim approximately*

¾ *inch.* With right sides together, sew short ends of band together. Grade seam allowances. **Note:** *When pinning band to the sweatshirt, long side of graded seam allowance should face the front of the garment.*

13. Measure button width and add ⅛ inch for length of buttonhole. Stitch right sides of band together for this length approximately ¾ inch above right end of collar band (Figure 8). Turn collar band to the right side.

Figure 8

14. Mark center of collar band. Pin one layer of right side of band to wrong side of jacket neckline at each end of neckline, at each shoulder and at center back of jacket. Gently stretch and pin band between center back and shoulders to ease in for a snug fit. Stitch collar in place. Press seam allowance toward collar. Press collar, allowing remaining raw edge to lie flat on right side of jacket (it will be covered with snap tape).

15. To face the raw edge at buttonhole, cut a piece of batik fabric the length of the buttonhole plus ½ inch by 2 inches wide. Press under ¼ inch on three sides. Place facing on outside of collar at buttonhole and pin in place with raw edge extending ⅝ inch over seam line. Hand-stitch into place.

16. Stitch the male section of snap tape over edges of collar. Turn under ends and stitch by hand. Couch-stitch chenille yarn between the edge of the snap tape and the banded collar, leaving long ends; use a darning needle to pull ends inside collar band. Along the opposite edge of the tape and extending along the edge of the batik bias strips to the bottom edges of fronts, stitch two layers of ¼-inch bias strips of dupioni.

17. Sew on button opposite buttonhole using strands of yarn. ❖

Sources: Authentic Pigment sweatshirt, HTC Fusible Tailors Tape from www.londas-sewing.com; variegated heavy silk thread from Clover Needlecrafts Inc.

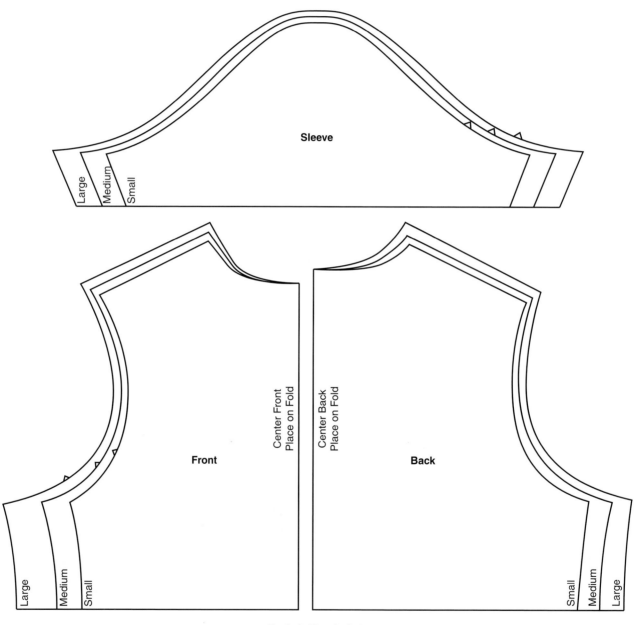

Sleeve

Large
Medium
Small

Front

Center Front
Place on Fold

Center Back
Place on Fold

Back

Large
Medium
Small

Small
Medium
Large

Fuchsia Fun Jacket
Templates
Enlarge 400%

Bolero Vest

BY ELIZABETH HILL FOR COATS & CLARK

Create this snappy vest from a plain-Jane sweatshirt.

FINISHED SIZE
Your size

MATERIALS
- Sweatshirt with set-in sleeves
- 44/45-inch-wide black solid cotton fabric for lining:
  - ¾ yard for small/medium
  - 1½ yards for large/extra-large
- 2 packages black double-wide bias tape
- Coats & Clark Dual Duty XP thread:
  - black #900
  - pink #1840
  - blue #9255
- 2 small black frog closures
- Fabric stabilizer suitable for knits
- Quilter's tape
- Basic sewing supplies and equipment

PROJECT NOTES
Refer to model project photo for stitch and placement ideas.

Use black thread in bobbin.

Use stabilizer behind all rows of decorative stitching to avoid puckering.

Staystitch ¼ inch from all cut edges.

DESIGN & ASSEMBLY

1. Select, prewash and press sweatshirt as suggested in General Instructions on page 4.

2. Referring to Cutting Instructions (page 5), remove ribbing from sweatshirt neck and bottom edges; mark front centerline and cut open.

3. Determine how deep and wide you want the scoop of the neckline to be and make a paper pattern (see neckline curve template, page 15). Mark neckline with chalk, and cut.

4. Remove sleeves from sweatshirt. Measure 1½–2 inches from outside edge at top seam and mark with a pin. Taper with a curved line from this pin to the bottom of the armhole (see armhole curve template, page 15). Cut armholes.

5. Trim hem of sweatshirt to fall at the natural waistline. **Note:** *Model project was cut 3 inches from top of ribbing (new hemline).* Curve edges of top and bottom opening (see corner template, page 15). **Option:** *Leave corners square and miter bias tape at corners.*

6. Gently remove shoulder seam stitches.

7. Measure 1½ inches down from inside corner of neckline curve. Place quilter's tape from sleeve edge to vest opening along this measurement. Using tape as a guide, use satin stitch to make the horizontal vest yoke. Mark and stitch the yoke on the back to match the vest front.

8. Experiment with decorative stitches or a combination of utility stitches to create thread stripes on the front and back of the vest. A 2.5mm double needle was used on the model project with contrasting threads. A single needle may be used. Record all stitch settings for easy reference as you sew.

9. Decide how many rows of stripes you want on each side of the vest and across the back. **Note:** *The model project has three rows on each front panel and eight rows across the back, spaced 2 inches apart.* Measure and mark with quilter's tape. Start vertical rows of stitching from the top down. Carefully put needle into the fabric directly below the thread yoke line, sewing down to the hem. Pull threads to the back and tie.

10. To make diamond design above the thread yoke, use the diamond template (page 15) to cut two patterns. Measure 3½ inches down from the center of the shoulder seam for the first diamond and pin in place. Place the second diamond ¼ inch directly below the first. Stitch a figure eight around the diamonds using a long straight stitch. Secure threads on the back. Repeat on the opposite front.

ASSEMBLY

1. With wrong sides together, place open vest on top of lining fabric and pin in place. Cut out. Stitch together around all edges using a ¼-inch seam allowance (Figure 1). ***Note:*** *For small/ medium size, place vest on lining selvage to selvage; for large/extra-large size, place vest lengthwise on lining fabric.*

Figure 1

2. With right sides together, stitch front to back at shoulder seams. Finish seams with zigzag or overcast stitches. Clip curves.

3. Bind edges with double-fold bias tape.

4. Attach one frog above the thread yoke and one frog below the yoke following manufacturer's instructions. ❖

Source: Thread from Coats & Clark.

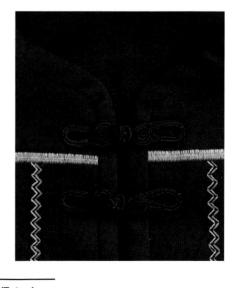

Top Edge

Corner

Bottom Edge

Diamond

Armhole Curve

Neckline Curve for Small/Medium

Neckline Curve for Large/Extra Large

Bolero Vest
Templates
Actual size

Black & White

BY LORINE MASON

Make a dramatic statement with this black-and-white jacket.

FINISHED SIZE
Your size

MATERIALS
- Black crewneck sweatshirt with set-in sleeves
- ½ yard black-and-white floral print cotton fabric
- ¼ yard white solid cotton fabric
- 4 yards ¼-inch-wide black-and-white check ribbon
- ¼ yard fusible interfacing
- ¼ yard fusible web
- ¼-inch-wide fusible web tape
- Basic sewing supplies and equipment

DESIGN & ASSEMBLY
Note: *Use ¼-inch seam allowance unless otherwise stated.*

1. Select, prewash and press sweatshirt as suggested in General Instructions on page 4.

2. Referring to Cutting Instructions (page 5), remove ribbing from sweatshirt cuffs and bottom edges; mark front centerline and cut open.

3. Measure 7 inches from neckline band at center front edge. Mark this point with a pin (Figure 1). Starting at the pin, cut a curve toward the neckline ribbing, cutting away the ribbing from around the neckline. Use the trimmed front edge as a pattern to duplicate the curve on the opposite front side.

Figure 1

4. Fold sweatshirt in half, matching front edges. Measure 7 inches from bottom at center back and mark with a pin. Cut through both layers of the sweatshirt, starting at the 7-inch pin mark and angling the cut down toward the center front bottom edge (Figure 2).

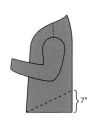

Figure 2

5. Press fusible web tape to the wrong side of the neckline and the front and bottom edges of the sweatshirt. Remove paper backing and turn edges of sweatshirt under ¼ inch. Press well. Pin ribbon to right side of sweatshirt along the neckline and the front and bottom edges. Stitch through all layers along both edges of the ribbon.

6. Press fusible web to the wrong side of the print fabric. Choose several of the floral motifs from the print fabric and cut around each. Referring to Appliqué Techniques on page 7, appliqué floral motifs and flowerpot (using template on page 18) to front of sweatshirt. Add stems and leaves with satin stitch.

7. Measure bottom edge of sleeve. Add 1 inch to this measurement. Use sleeve measurement to adjust cuff template (page 18) as needed. Using template, cut two cuffs from black-and-white floral print, two from white solid and two from interfacing. Press interfacing to the wrong side of the white cuff sections. With right sides together, sew one white and one black-and-white cuff together along side and bottom edges (Figure 3). Fold raw edges under ¼ inch and press.

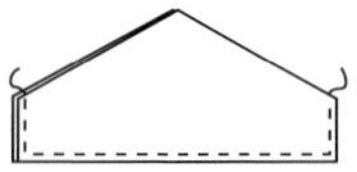

Figure 3

HOUSE OF WHITE BIRCHES, BERNE, INDIANA 46711   DRGNETWORK.COM

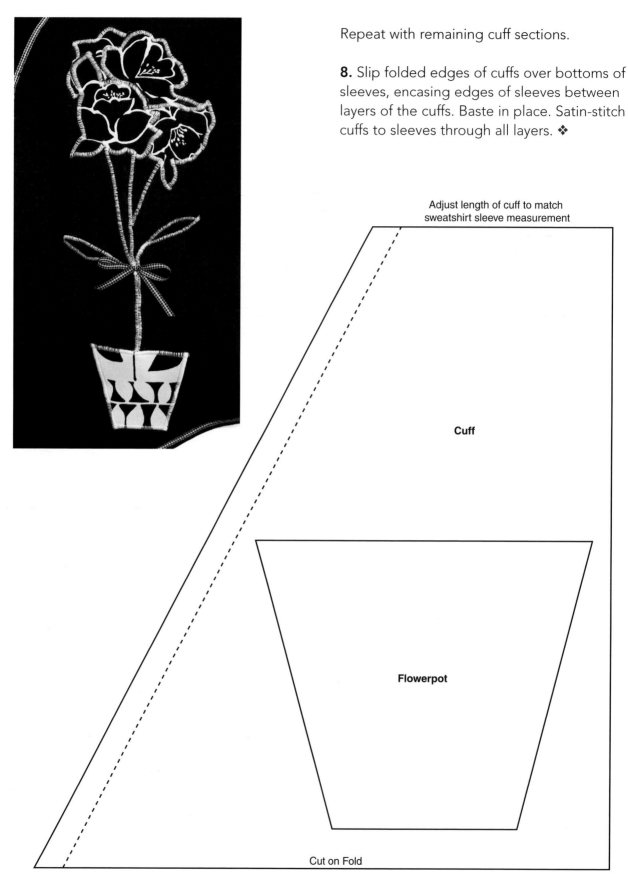

Repeat with remaining cuff sections.

8. Slip folded edges of cuffs over bottoms of sleeves, encasing edges of sleeves between layers of the cuffs. Baste in place. Satin-stitch cuffs to sleeves through all layers. ❖

Adjust length of cuff to match
sweatshirt sleeve measurement

Cuff

Flowerpot

Cut on Fold

Black & White
Templates
Actual size

Tailored Tapestry

BY MISSY SHEPLER

Dress up a simple sweatshirt design with home-dec fabrics.

FINISHED SIZE
Your size

MATERIALS
- Sweatshirt with set-in sleeves
- 26 x 26 inches lightweight home-dec fabric
- ½ yard 22-inch-wide lightweight fusible interfacing
- Coordinating yarn for embellishing
- 5 decorative buttons
- Braiding foot
- Basic sewing supplies and equipment

CUTTING
From home-dec fabric:
Enlarge collar and pocket templates (page 21) as indicated.
- Cut two collars, reversing one.
- Cut two pockets, reversing one.
- Cut two rectangles 5 inches wide by the length of the sweatshirt plus 4 inches for facing/lapel.

From lightweight fusible interfacing:
- Use enlarged template to cut one collar.
- Cut two rectangles 4¾ inches wide by the length of the sweatshirt plus 4 inches for facing/lapel.

DESIGN & ASSEMBLY
Note: *Use ¼-inch seam allowance unless otherwise stated.*

1. Select, prewash and press sweatshirt as suggested in General Instructions on page 4.

2. Referring to Cutting Instructions (page 5), remove ribbing from sweatshirt neckline, cuffs and bottom edges; mark front centerline and cut open.

3. Try on sweatshirt. Mark desired sleeve and jacket lengths. Cut off, allowing for ¾-inch hem for sleeves and 1-inch hem for jacket. Finish cut edges with zigzag or overlock stitches.

4. Fuse collar interfacing to wrong side of one fabric collar. Place fabric collars right sides together and stitch around outer edges, pivoting at corners and leaving neck edge open. Trim and grade seam allowances at collar points (Figure 1).

Figure 1

5. Turn collar right side out. Press. Test-fit collar on sweatshirt neck edge, matching center backs. Pin-mark sweatshirt neck edge at collar end points. Remove collar.

6. Matching one long edge, fuse interfacing facing/lapel to wrong side of each fabric facing/lapel. Press under ¼ inch of fabric and stitch to finish (Figure 2).

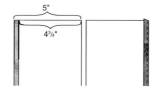

Figure 2

7. With right sides together, align unfinished facing/lapel edge with sweatshirt front edge, extending facing lapel slightly past collar end point at neck edge. Pin neck and collar edges. Stitch along neck edge and sweatshirt front, pivoting at lapel corner and ending at pin-mark

for the collar end points (Figure 3). Trim excess lapel lining at neck edge. Trim and grade seam allowances at corner points. Trim excess facing length to match sweatshirt front lower edge. Turn facing/lapel to wrong side of sweatshirt; press. Repeat for opposite side.

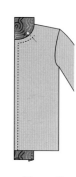

Figure 3

8. With right sides together, pin one layer of collar to neck edge, matching center backs and catching unstitched lapel edge within seam. Stitch collar to sweatshirt at neck edge. Press a ¼-inch seam allowance toward collar. Fold under ¼ inch along remaining collar raw neck edge and press. Machine- or hand-stitch collar seam, enclosing raw edges.

9. On jacket front, mark a vertical buttonhole approximately 6 inches from neckline and ¾ inch from front edge. Stitch buttonhole and sew on button. **Note:** *Lightweight interfacing provides extra stability for buttonhole openings.* Use a small button on the wrong side of the sweatshirt to add support for the button.

10. On each sleeve, fold under ¾ inch along sleeve edge. On right side of sleeve edge, couch-stitch decorative yarn ½ inch from bottom edge, beginning and ending stitching at sleeve seam. Tuck sleeve seam into a 1-inch pleat and hand-stitch through all layers to anchor. Cover stitching with a decorative button.

11. Mark sweatshirt right side seam 7 inches from bottom. Stitch ⅛ inch along both sides and across top of marked line. Cut between stitching along marked line and finish cut edges with zigzag or overlock stitching.

12. With right sides together, align pocket pieces along cut line, placing point A on pocket ¼ inch above upper end of cut line. Stitch pocket pieces to sweatshirt along cut line (Figure 4). Couch-stitch decorative yarn down front edge of pocket, being careful not to catch pocket in stitching. If desired, leave a long end of yarn at top of pocket for tying on decorative buttons. Turn pocket pieces to wrong side of sweatshirt.

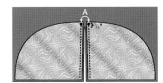

Figure 4

11. On wrong side of sweatshirt, place pocket pieces right sides together, aligning edges. Stitch pieces together around pocket edges, leaving sweatshirt edges open to form pocket. Zigzag or overlock edges to finish. On sweatshirt right side, press pocket edges.

12. Turn under a 1-inch hem on facing and sweatshirt bottom edges, encasing pocket bottom seam inside hem. Press. Stitch ½ inch from folded edge to secure. Fold facing to wrong side and hand-stitch in place across bottom to finish. ❖

Sources: Dragon Tale rayon slub yarn from The Weavers Loft; fusible interfacing from Pellon Consumer Products.

FUN FEET!

Getting started on the right foot makes all the difference. Taking a few moments to learn to use the attachments that come with your machine, or specialty options that are available, can curb sewing frustrations and lead to future time savings!

Overlock Foot—A small pin on the right side of this foot helps keep fabric flat and prevents tunneling to create a smooth finished edge.

Braiding Foot—A hole in the base of this foot acts as a guide for thick cord or yarn, making it easy to couch down extra embellishments on any project.

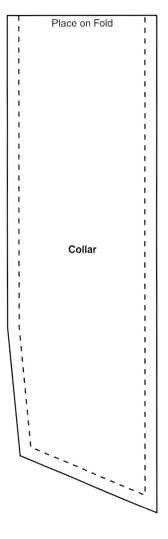

Place on Fold

Collar

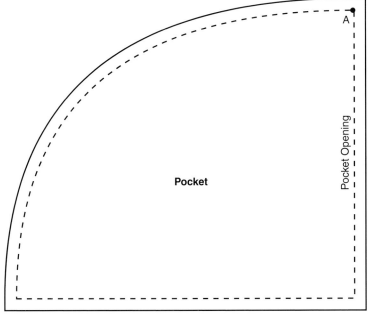

Pocket

Pocket Opening

A

Tailored Tapestry Jacket
Templates
Enlarge 200%

Felted Vest

BY LAURA KEITH

The colors of the sky, sunset, sand and sea foam provide the color palette, while decorative thread adds texture.

FINISHED SIZE
Your size

MATERIALS
- White cotton sweatshirt with set-in sleeves
- Decorative fabric and fibers:
    - 2 ounces white for background color*
    - 1 ounce turquoise and orange*
    - neutral-tone silk or wool/wool blend fiber
    - ½ yard silk organza or silk chiffon scraps
    - peach silk/rayon decorative thread
- Fusible hologramic fiber, fused onto a sheet per manufacturer's instructions
- Decorative yarn or cord for couching
- 1 (1¼–1⅜-inch) shell button
- 1 (¾-inch) bar pin back
- Needle-felting tool
- Foam pad at least 12 x 12 x 2 inches
- Unused coir-fiber welcome mat
- Spray bottle
- Hand-dishwashing detergent
- Cotton muslin sheeting:
    - 2 squares adequate to cover the vest body
    - small piece to cover lapels
- Nonskid rubber shelf-liner webbing in same size as muslin sheeting
- 3 (12-inch) elastic ties
- Plastic washtub
- Large tray with lip
- Fusible hem tape
- Basic sewing supplies and equipment

*Mulberry silk and wool blend were used in model project.

PROJECT NOTE
To allow for slight shrinkage that will occur during the wet-felting process, select a sweatshirt that is loose-fitting or slightly large.

DESIGN & ASSEMBLY
1. Select, prewash and press sweatshirt as suggested in General Instructions on page 4.

2. Referring to Cutting Instructions (page 5), cut off sleeves and seams at the armholes. Cut off bottom ribbing and seam, and neck ribbing and seam. Measure across the shoulders to be sure they are the same width. Mark front centerline and cut open.

3. Try on the vest to check for fit; trim as needed. Determine the point at which the front neckline will fold back to form the lapel and pin in place. Trim neckline as needed. Lay sweatshirt on the coir-fiber mat with the front panels meeting at the center front.

4. Cut out the silk fabric and the fusible hologramic fiber into ½-inch-wide strips of various lengths. Stagger the lengths as you lay them out vertically and evenly spaced across the front panels: Place a 7-inch length a few inches from the front edge and a 9- or 10-inch length further away toward the side seam (Figure 1).

Figure 1

HOUSE OF WHITE BIRCHES, BERNE, INDIANA 46711   DRGNETWORK.COM

TIPS & TECHNIQUES

Don't be afraid to overlap colors, as they will blend together during the felting process. Placing white fibers over bright fibers will tend to mute and soften them, creating a watercolor effect.

5. Continue laying out decorative fabric, threads and fiber strips in a pleasing design, keeping in mind that any non-wool fiber needs to be covered with a wool fiber. Draw out a few long wisps of the orange-color fiber and lay it vertically on the right front panel; add a shorter wisp of the same color to the left front panel. Do the same for the other colors. Continue the design up the lengths of the front panels.

6. Lay out wisps of the white fiber over non-wool elements, including threads and fabrics. Place the white wool sparingly wherever you want to secure a thread, fabric or fiber, continuing the white wool onto the upper part of the front as well (Figure 2). Lay down as much or as little as you like. **Note:** *Lay white fiber on the front panel under the lapel and on the fleece side of the lapel, but not on the underside of the lapel.*

Figure 2

TIPS & TECHNIQUES

As you design, don't hesitate to replace any unwanted fiber or thread with another. You may even wish to leave the work and come back to it at a later time.

7. Gently lift up sweatshirt and place foam pad under front panels only. Use needle-felting tool to felt fibers, following manufacturer's instructions. Needle-felt lapels in same manner.

8. Open out front panels and turn sweatshirt over so back side is facing up (Figure 3). Lay down white fiber to cover back as desired. Needle-felt thoroughly, placing shoulders on the foam mat and needle-felting over the seam line to meet the fiber on the front and back panels, and doing the same at the sides.

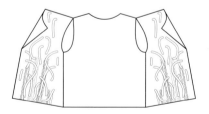

Figure 3

WET-FELTING

1. Return sweatshirt to position of Figure 3. Place in tray. Soak both muslin pieces thoroughly with tap water and place one piece (this will be the back panel) on top of the sweatshirt. Place the shelf liner on top of the muslin and another layer of muslin over the liner.

2. Fold the front panels of the sweatshirt so center front edges meet. Place small piece of muslin over embellished sides of the lapels. **Note:** *The reverse (fleece) side of the front of the sweatshirt should be facing up, then the muslin, then the shelf liner, another layer of muslin and then the back of the sweatshirt on the bottom.*

3. Fill spray bottle half full with water. Add a teaspoon of hand-dishwashing detergent. Spray fabric with the detergent solution and massage the fleece side of the fabric where the fibers show through, spraying often to prevent drying out. Continue working until fibers begin to felt into sweatshirt. (The fibers will be tightly bound to the face of the fabric and will resist a gentle pinch.) Repeat the process with the lapels and then flip the sweatshirt and repeat for the back.

4. Remove the shelf liner. Roll up the sweatshirt and muslin layers, and tie with elastic ties.

5. Fill the plastic tub with lukewarm water and dunk bundle into water, squeezing water through it. Repeat with successively hotter water, unrolling and checking between dunkings. To prevent excessive shrinking, limit the number of dunkings to two or three. Finish with a final dunk and rinse in cold water. Unwrap the vest and lay flat to dry.

FINISHING

1. Turn neckline, front, armhole and lower hem edges ⅜–½ inch wrong side out and pin. **Note:** *Leave lapels free; they will be finished independently.* Trim edges where needed and measure all around to be sure hemline is even and lapels match up. Pin-mark the top and bottom points of the lapels (Figure 4).

Figure 4

2. Measure a length of decorative yarn or cord for couching to go around the lapel plus 10 inches. With matching embroidery or polyester thread in the machine needle and polyester bobbin thread, begin at the top or bottom point of the lapel to couch the yarn with a zigzag stitch ⅛ inch from the raw edge, leaving a 5-inch tail at beginning and end (Figure 5). **Note:** *Yarn is couched through only a single layer on the lapel.* Repeat on opposite lapel.

Figure 5

3. Finish neckline and armhole edges in same manner, couching yarn through two layers of sweatshirt and maintaining the same distance from edge so line appears unbroken all around.

4. Open out lower front corners and snip out a square of fabric from the bottom hem under each front edge to eliminate bulk in the front corner (Figure 6).

Figure 6

5. Re-pin hem. Line up the sewing machine foot and the couching yarn with yarn path at bottom of lapel as before. Couch to the corner, turn and continue along lower hem around and up the opposite side of the front, ending at the opposite lower lapel point.

6. Fuse small pieces of fusible hem tape between layers of sweatshirt fabric at lower right and left front corners. Zigzag-stitch the overlap.

7. Cut a narrow strip of silk organza approximately 18 inches long. Insert ends through holes in button from front to back. Open pin back and insert ends through holes on pin back. Tie ends tightly and knot, securing pin back to back of button. Pin front of vest below lapels to close. ❖

Sources: Wool/wool blend and silk fiber from Crown Mountain Farms; silk organza, silk chiffon and cotton muslin from Dharma Trading Co.; Angelina fusible hologramic fiber from The Button Emporium and Ribbonry; felting needles, wool/wool blend and silk fiber from Woodland Woolworks.

THE FINER POINTS OF NEEDLE FELTING

Not so long ago, felting needles were used exclusively in industrial felt making. Thousands of them were inserted into a holder and used to punch unspun fibers like wool, cotton and polyester until they became matted into feltlike material. Each needle has notches cut into the blade which catch on the fiber as the needle passes through.

As more U.S. textile production has been exported, many of these needles have become creative tools for the textile and fiber artist. Because the wool fiber cuticle is made up of tiny scales, it is particularly suited to be felted with needles and also with agitation, soap and water.

Needle felting is very simple. Protect yourself from the sharp needle by placing your project on a thick foam surface and then on a stable surface such as a table or countertop. Locate the fiber you wish to catch and then jab the needle down on the fiber and through the base fabric. Continue this motion on the surrounding fibers along the length of the project. Multiple pokes produce more securely embedded fibers.

Many projects require only this process to anchor the fibers, especially if they are placed densely in a small area, and the item will not receive heavy wear. Multiple-needle tools save wear on the hand and wrist, and are for sale at craft stores throughout the country. Unspun wool fiber, or roving, is becoming available in craft stores where the needle-felting supplies are displayed and is often packaged in kits of several bright colors. **Note:** *Avoid superwash fiber, as it has been pretreated to resist felting.*

TIPS & TECHNIQUES

If garment shape becomes slightly distorted, you may be able to restore it by gently pulling the couched thread to reduce the distortion. Note: This can be done only if you have not stitched through the couching yarn.

Twisted-Vine Hoodie

BY DIANE BUNKER

Use two sweatshirts to create a unique peekaboo appliqué.

FINISHED SIZE
Your size

MATERIALS
- 2 identical hooded zippered sweatshirts (in brand and size) in sage green and black or other contrasting colors
- ½ yard 36-inch-wide white-on-white print fabric
- Fabric painting medium
- Acrylic paints in 7 coordinating colors to complement sweatshirts
- Multicolored quilting thread
- Rayon embroidery thread in contrasting color
- Chalk
- White watercolor pencil
- Freehand or darning foot
- Small sharp scissors
- Basic sewing supplies and equipment

PROJECT NOTES
Refer to your owner's manual for how to lower the feed dogs for freehand-motion sewing.

See back cover for reverse side of hoodie design.

PAINTED FABRIC
1. Wash, dry and press fabric. Lay flat on protected surface.

2. Mix an equal part fabric painting medium with first-color paint and thin slightly with water. Beginning at one edge of fabric, paint a 5-inch-wide stripe completely across the ½-yard length. Repeat with each color. Let dry completely.

3. Cut out each colored strip. Fold in half lengthwise, wrong sides together, so each strip is 2½ x 18 inches. Use leaf template (page 28) to cut five pairs of leaves from each doubled strip. **Note:** *Each leaf is doubled when pinned between the shirts.*

DESIGN & ASSEMBLY
1. Select, prewash and press sweatshirts as suggested in General Instructions on page 4.

2. Enlarge vine template (page 28) as indicated and trace onto pattern tracing paper. Chalk the back of the tracing, and then lay the chalked tracing in place on the darker sweatshirt. Rub over the design to transfer it onto the sweatshirt; go over transferred chalk lines with a white watercolor pencil, dampening the pencil tip for drawing ease.

3. Fit sweatshirts with wrong sides together and pin loosely. Pin leaves in place between sweatshirts. **Note:** *Some leaves will overlap a bit, so determine when to sandwich a leaf into another leaf so when the sweatshirt is cut away only one leaf color shows through.*

4. Using multicolored quilting thread in needle and bobbin, attach the freehand foot and drop the feed dogs. Freehand-sew the design, starting at the top of the darker sweatshirt, stitching down one side and then the other. For the swirls, sew to the end of the swirl, and then follow the pattern back to the start of the swirl. Keep it loose and try not to stay on the same line on the way back. The leaves are outlined only once for now. Try to keep the design flowing without stopping and starting.

5. Cut out center of each leaf using small sharp scissors, being careful not to cut painted fabric. Make sure no raw leaf edges are showing. Change needle thread to rayon embroidery thread. Sew the design again on contrasting sweatshirt side, keeping it slightly off for a freehand look.

6. If desired, shade each leaf using a darker value of each color with the fabric medium. Let dry. ***Note:*** *Sweatshirts are sewn together along vine design only.* ❖

Source: Fabric painting medium #DSA10 and Americana Acrylics paints from Deco Art.

Zipper Edge

Top Section

Leaf

Pocket

Bottom Section

Middle Section

Twisted Vine Hoodie
Templates
Enlarge 200%

Coco & Camelot

BY SHEILA ZENT

This timeless jacket-and-skirt ensemble was inspired by the tailored suits designed by Coco Chanel.

FINISHED SIZE
Your size

MATERIALS
- Sweatshirts with set-in sleeves:
    - 1 in predominant color, sized to fit (A)
    - 1 in same color, 1 size larger (B)
    - 1 in contrasting color, same size as shirt B (C)
- Separating sport zipper with plastic teeth (see step 3 for length)
- Optional: ½- or ¾-inch-wide elastic to fit waist measurement with overlap
- Basic sewing supplies and equipment

DESIGN & ASSEMBLY
Note: Use ¼-inch seam allowance unless otherwise stated.

1. Select, prewash and press sweatshirts as suggested in General Instructions on page 4.

2. For jacket, place sweatshirt A on work surface. Referring to Cutting Instructions (page 5), remove ribbing from sweatshirt neck, cuff and bottom edges; mark front centerline and cut open. Edge-finish raw edges with serging or zigzagging.

Figure 1

Optional: Try on shirt and pin out excess along side and underarm seams for a more tailored fit as desired. Stitch and trim away excess fabric (Figure 1).

3. Measure length of center front edge and subtract 1½ inches to allow for neck and bottom hems. Round this measurement down to the nearest even number to determine zipper length.

4. Press under ¼ inch to wrong sides along both center front edges. Mark ½ inch from top corner and 1 inch from lower corner on each side. Center zipper between marks and pin folded edge to outside of zipper teeth. Edgestitch in place.

5. Press under ½ inch around neckline and topstitch ⅜ inch from the fold. Press under 1 inch along bottom hem and topstitch ¾ inch from fold.

6. Try on jacket to determine sleeve length. Mark 2 inches above desired length on each sleeve. Trim excess length evenly from bottoms of both sleeves. Set aside.

7. For skirt, place sweatshirt B on work surface with bottom ribbing at the top. Trim off sleeves to the outside of the armscye seam. Measure 17 inches from the ribbing seam toward the neckline on the shirt; mark and cut (Figure 2, page 30). **Note:** *Model project measures 19 inches from the waist to the finished hem. For longer or shorter skirt, adjust measurements* *accordingly before cutting.* Turn skirt wrong side out. Pin sides to fit and close up armscye area (Figure 3). Stitch, trim seam allowance and finish raw edges. Set skirt aside.

Figure 2   Figure 3

8. Place sweatshirt C on work surface. Cut off ribbing from hem and sleeves and trim edges even. From body of the shirt, cut a continuous strip 6 inches wide (Figure 4). With right sides together, stitch one edge to the skirt hem edge, seaming the strip as needed so that the edges fit equally. Press under opposite side ½ inch. Pin folded edge to wrong side of the skirt in the same manner as a waistband. Hand- or machine-stitch in the ditch.

Figure 4

9. If skirt waistband is too large, fold waist ribbing in half and stitch ribbing fold to the original seam allowance to create a casing. Insert elastic to draw in the waist and stitch ends together to fit comfortably.

10. Measure around the bottom of the jacket sleeves. Add 1 inch to this measurement. Cut one or both sleeves from shirt C and slit along seam to open flat. Cut two strips for sleeve bands, each as long as the measurement and 6 inches wide. Stitch short seams together and attach bands to bottom of each sleeve, finishing in same manner as the bottom skirt band.

11. Measure jacket edge from center back, around the neck edge and down the center front to the hem. Add 10 inches to this measurement.

Using this measurement, cut 2-inch-wide strips as follows: four from shirt C and two from remains of shirt B.

12. With right sides together, fold each strip in half lengthwise and stitch the long edge with a scant ½-inch seam allowance; turn right side out. Braid together one matching and two contrasting strips. At one end of each braid, finish strips by tucking raw edges to inside and hand-stitching. Repeat to make two braids.

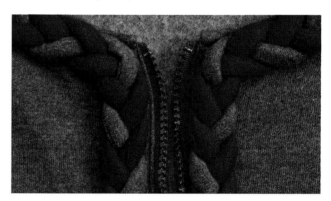

13. Starting at the center back neckline, hand-stitch braids to each side of the jacket neckline and down the front edges to each side of the zipper. Trim and finish opposite ends of each braid at the bottom hem. Join braid ends together at the nape of the neckline.

Figure 5

14. Cut two faux pocket welts each 6½ x 4 inches from remains of shirt C. Fold in half lengthwise and stitch raw edges together, leaving a 2-inch opening along each long edge. Turn right sides out and press. Position on jacket front as desired. Topstitch along side and bottom edges (Figure 5). Press. ❖

Two-Sided Sweatshirt

BY JANIS BULLIS

You'll grab this versatile cover-up every time you venture outside.

FINISHED SIZE
Your size

MATERIALS
- 2 identical sweatshirts (in brand and size) in coordinating colors with set-in sleeves
- 2 (5-yard) packages extra-wide double-fold bias tape
- 2 (5-yard) packages jumbo rickrack
- 5 yards 1¾-inch-wide flat lace
- 2 frog closures
- Basic sewing supplies and equipment

DESIGN & ASSEMBLY
1. Select, prewash and press sweatshirts as suggested in General Instructions on page 4.

2. Referring to Cutting Instructions (page 5), remove ribbing from each sweatshirt neck, cuff and bottom edges; mark front centerline and cut open. ***Note: Finished jacket features ¾ sleeve length. Cut sweatshirt sleeves 2 inches longer than desired finished sleeve length (Figure 1).***

Figure 1

3. Using the edge of a large mug or small saucer, round-off the corners at the neck and lower front.

4. Turn one sweatshirt inside out and slip it inside the other. Pin and baste all edges together (Figure 2).

Figure 2

5. With one scalloped edge along cut edge of jacket, pin and/or baste rickrack along all edges of one sweatshirt, seaming ends to join. ***Note: Because sleeves turn up to form a contrasting cuff, apply rickrack to edges of sleeves of opposite-color sweatshirt.***

6. Baste; then stitch narrow side of bias tape over rickrack along fold of tape, joining ends with a bias seam.

7. Repeat step 5 to attach lace to opposite-color sweatshirt. Fold bias tape over sweatshirt edges and hand-stitch in place to hide seam line.

8. Follow manufacturer's instructions to attach frog closures on both sides of sweatshirts. ❖

Swing on By

BY MISSY SHEPLER

Swing on by with turned-back cuffs and sassy patch pockets.

FINISHED SIZE
Your size

MATERIALS
- Sweatshirt with set-in sleeves
- 1 yard 44/45-inch-wide accent fabric
- 1 yard 22-inch-wide lightweight fusible interfacing
- Coordinating yarns, lace and other embellishment as desired
- 6½ x 7 inches batting
- 4 (⅝-inch) buttons
- Basic sewing supplies and equipment

CUTTING
From accent fabric:
- Cut two 6½-inch strips the width of the fabric for front linings.
- Cut one 5½ x 14-inch piece for back neck lining. **Note:** *Adjust length as needed for individual sweatshirt. Back neck lining should extend from shoulder seam to shoulder seam, matching ends of front lining pieces plus ¼ inch at each end for hem.*
- Cut two 6½-inch strips the circumference of the cuffs plus ½ inch.
- Cut one piece 11 inches by the length of the center back plus ¾ inch for the back inset panel.
- Cut two 6½ x 7-inch rectangles for pocket front and back.

From lightweight fusible interfacing:
- Cut two 6-inch-wide strips the length of the sweatshirt for front linings.
- Cut one 5½ x 14-inch piece for back neck lining, adjusting as needed (see cutting instructions for accent fabric).

DESIGN & ASSEMBLY
Note: *Use ¼-inch seam allowance unless otherwise stated.*

1. Select, prewash and press sweatshirt as suggested in General Instructions on page 4.

2. Referring to Cutting Instructions (page 5), remove ribbing from sweatshirt neckline, cuffs and bottom edges; mark front centerline and cut open. Reserve one cuff ribbing for pocket top.

3. Try on sweatshirt. Mark desired sleeve and jacket lengths. **Note:** *Allow approximately 1–1½ inches additional sleeve length for folding back cuffs.* Remove sweatshirt. Mark center back from 6 inches below neckline to sweatshirt lower edge. Stitch ⅛ inch from line on both sides and across top of marked line. Do not cut center back line at this time.

4. Finish all cut edges with zigzag or overlock stitch to prevent stretching and raveling.

5. Fuse one 6-inch-wide piece of interfacing to the wrong side of one front lining, matching edges on one long side and leaving ¼ inch of fabric exposed along one short edge. Repeat with remaining 6-inch-wide interfacing and front lining, making a mirror image of the first fused piece. Sew ¼-inch double hem in long edges (Figure 1).

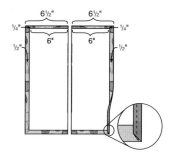

Figure 1

6. With right sides together, pin front lining edges to sweatshirt front, aligning unfinished edges of lining with sweatshirt front and neckline edges. Stitch along sweatshirt front and neckline edge, pivoting at corner. Trim excess lining at neck edge. Clip corner at neck edge and grade seam allowance at corner point. Trim excess lining at bottom edge, allowing ¼ inch for hem (Figure 2). Press under ¼ inch to wrong side of lining and stitch. Turn lining to inside and press. Repeat for opposite side.

Figure 2

7. Fuse interfacing to back neck lining. With right sides together, center and pin faced lining to back neck edge, extending lining above neck edge as needed to accommodate neckline curve (Figure 3). Stitch to neck edge. Trim excess lining above neck edge. Turn lining to inside. Press.

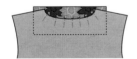

Figure 3

8. Using front facing end points as guides, cut side edges of back neck facing in a gentle curve, allowing for a ¼-inch hem; turn under and stitch. Hand-stitch front facings to back neck facing at shoulder seams.

9. With wrong sides together, press each cuff in half lengthwise. Open and press ¼ inch to wrong side along one long edge of each cuff. Edge-finish unpressed short end of cuff. With right sides together, stitch seam along short side of each cuff to form two short tubes (Figure 4). Finger-press seam allowances open.

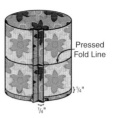

Pressed Fold Line

¼"

¼"

Figure 4

10. With wrong sides together and matching cuff seam to sweatshirt sleeve seam, tuck one edge-finished side of cuff inside one sleeve up to pressed fold line. Fold remaining side with pressed ¼-inch edge over outer side of sleeve, encasing sweatshirt sleeve inside fabric cuff. ***Note:*** *Make sure sweatshirt fills fold.* Pin. Stitch along folded ¼-inch edge on outside of sleeve to secure. Press. Repeat for opposite sleeve and cuff. Fold cuffs back to desired length.

11. Turn under ¼ inch on one 11-inch edge of back panel; stitch. Machine-baste ½ inch from this edge. On opposite 11-inch edge, turn under and stitch a double ¼-inch hem.

Cut center back of sweatshirt on marked line (step 3 of Design & Assembly). Zigzag or overlock cut edges.

12. With right sides together, stitch back inset panel to sweatshirt back, placing basted end of panel at top of sweatshirt-back cut and aligning long edges of panel and sweatshirt edges (Figure 5). On wrong side of sweatshirt, pull basting thread to gather top edge of panel. Flatten gathers at basting line to reduce bulk and secure with a line of stitching. Hand-stitch gathers to sweatshirt, taking care to hide stitches. On sweatshirt right side, sew a button at the top of the cut.

Figure 5

allowance of opening. Hand-stitch opening closed. Position pocket on jacket as desired and hand-stitch or topstitch in place. ❖

Sources: Fabric from Hoffman Fabrics; Pellon fusible interfacing from Pellon Consumer Products.

13. Using contrasting yarn and matching thread, couch-stitch yarn around front and neckline edges and around top edges of cuffs.

14. Mark three buttonholes on sweatshirt right front edge, starting approximately ⅝ inch from front edge and 1 inch below neck. Stitch buttonholes 2–2½ inches apart. Sew on buttons.

15. Hem sweatshirt even with back panel, encasing lower front linings in hem.

16. Layer pocket front right side up on top of batting. Embellish as desired. **Note:** *Model project was embellished using yarn couch-stitched in diagonal patterns with a length of lace added, and buttons and charm later sewn on.* Cut seam allowance from reserved cuff ribbing (step 2 of Design & Assembly) and open ribbing to lie flat. Zigzag or overlock raw edges to prevent raveling. If desired, couch-stitch a length of yarn along one edge to embellish.

17. With right sides together, sew embellished side of ribbing to top edge of pocket front. Sew opposite edge of ribbing to top edge of pocket back. Sew pocket front and back right sides together, rounding lower corners and leaving a 2-inch opening for turning. Trim and clip curves. Turn right side out and press, folding in seam

Sophisticated Swirls

BY JANICE LOEWENTHAL

Create felted-wool paisleys, add some seed beads, and embellish a border to create a one-of-a-kind jacket.

FINISHED SIZE
Your size

MATERIALS
- Sweatshirt with set-in sleeves
- Wool or wool felt*:
    - ¼ yard dark coordinating color
    - ⅛ yard light coordinating color
- 1 package double-folded bias tape to coordinate with sweatshirt
- ⅛ yard fabric stabilizer
- 1 skein black pearl cotton
- 1 tube light green rocaille or seed beads
- 2 tubes black E beads
- Beading needle
- Freezer paper
- Basic sewing supplies and equipment

*Model project was made using wool felt.

PAISLEY APPLIQUÉS
Paisley appliqués can be made of either wool or wool felt. Wool needs no preparation, but wool felt must be preshrunk as follows:

1. Wash wool felt using hot water. Wash each color separately to avoid bleeding. Make sure it is soaked through, moving it around briskly 30 seconds or so—any longer and felt may become over-stretched.

2. Dry in dryer with a couple of old towels until nearly dry. Remove and smooth out with hands. Lay flat to complete drying.

DESIGN & ASSEMBLY
1. Select, prewash and press sweatshirt as suggested in General Instructions on page 4.

2. Referring to Cutting Instructions (page 5), remove ribbing from sweatshirt neck, cuff and bottom edges; mark front centerline and cut open.

Figure 1

3. Trace the scallop template and corner template (page 40) onto a piece of stabilizer.

4. Smooth sweatshirt onto a flat surface. Position the corner scallop template onto the right front (Figure 1). Use scallop template to mark scallops along the center front of the shirt, ending at the neck (Figure 2). Turn templates over and repeat on opposite side of shirt (Figure 3). **Note:** *Number of scallops will vary depending on size of sweatshirt.*

Figure 2

Figure 3

5. Align the scallop template with the edge of the corner template at the bottom edge of the shirt and mark scallops across the bottom edge. Repeat on opposite side (Figure 4) and

Figure 4

continue scallops across back, adjusting so scallops fit evenly. Trim on marked lines.

6. Sew one edge of bias tape as close as possible to raw edge of the shirt, beginning at the center back. Continue around the shirt, joining ends in the back. Repeat around edges of sleeves. Press and turn remaining edges to underside of shirt and hand-stitch in place.

7. Count the scallops around the shirt to determine the number of paisley pieces needed. Trace that number of paisley templates onto the dull side of freezer paper. ***Note:*** *Large and small paisley pieces are cut from darker felt; medium paisley pieces are cut from lighter felt.* Press the shiny side of paper onto the wool or wool felt using the wool setting. Using sharp scissors, cut out the paisley pieces and peel off the paper.

8. Using black pearl cotton, blanket-stitch a medium paisley onto a large paisley; then blanket-stitch a small paisley onto a medium paisley. Hand-stitch rocaille or seed beads onto small paisley until it is covered.

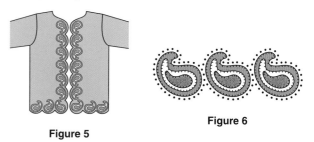

Figure 5

Figure 6

9. Position paisleys at each scallop (Figure 5) and blanket-stitch around each large paisley to attach to the shirt. Sew black E beads around each paisley as shown in Figure 6, sewing beads approximately ⅛ inch from outer edge of paisley at ¼-inch intervals. ❖

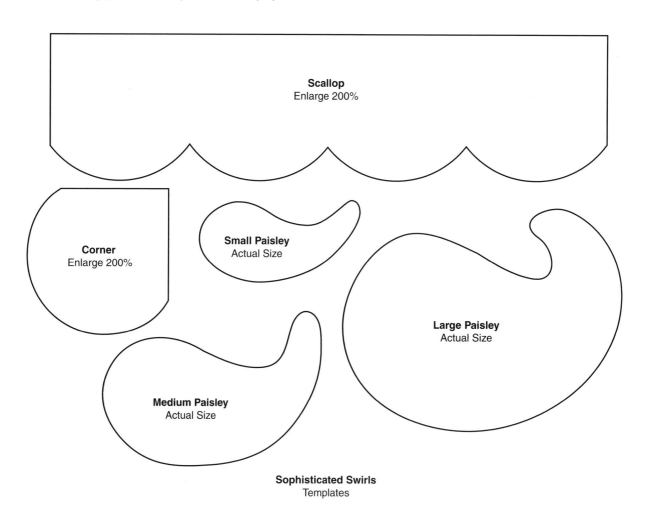

Scallop
Enlarge 200%

Corner
Enlarge 200%

Small Paisley
Actual Size

Large Paisley
Actual Size

Medium Paisley
Actual Size

Sophisticated Swirls
Templates

Grommet Accents

BY CAROL ZENTGRAF

Create a tunic with V-neck shaping, bias edges and grommet accents.

FINISHED SIZE
Your size

MATERIALS
- Sweatshirt with set-in sleeves
- 43 brass grommets with ⅜-inch openings*
- Grommet pliers
- 2 yards ⅜-inch-wide matching woven ribbon*
- 2 packages 1-inch-wide single-fold bias tape*
- Fusible tricot knit interfacing
- ½-inch-wide double-stick fusible web tape
- Permanent fabric adhesive
- Basic sewing supplies and equipment

*Model project is an adult size small sweatshirt. Larger sizes may require additional quantities.

DESIGN & ASSEMBLY
1. Select, prewash and press sweatshirt as suggested in General Instructions on page 4.

2. Referring to Cutting Instructions (page 5), remove ribbing from sweatshirt neckline, cuffs and bottom edges.

3. Mark 2 inches from neck edge on each shoulder seam and mark center front at desired depth. Draw lines from shoulder-seam marks to the center point (Figure 1). On the back, draw a line from one shoulder-seam mark to the other, shaping neckline in a slight curve. Cut shoulder seams open to marks and slit from neck edge to center point.

4. Cut strips of interfacing to fit neck opening. Fuse facing to wrong side of shirt. Fold front and back neck edges to inside along marked lines and pin in place. Edgestitch along neckline to secure.

5. To add bias trim, cut a piece of bias tape long enough to make a V around the front neckline with the outer edges of the V 1½ inches past the neck edges and extending ½ inch over the shoulder seams (Figure 1). Apply fusible

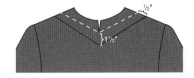

Figure 1

web tape to wrong side of bias tape (Figure 2). Position tape around neckline, mitering at the center, and fuse in place. Edgestitch along each edge of the bias tape. Repeat for back neckline, cutting bias tape to fit 1 inch from the neckline from shoulder seam to shoulder seam and adding 1 inch to the length. Turn each end under ½ inch and fuse; stitch in place, covering the raw ends of the front binding strips.

←Fusible Web Tape

Figure 2

6. Place shirt flat and mark side edges by pressing. Cut a 6-inch slit from lower edge of shirt along each side. Open bias tape and apply fusible web to wrong side as shown in Figure 2. Press under one end of the bias tape. Place this at the top of one slit edge on the front of the shirt, aligning the fused edge of the bias tape with the slit edge and wrapping the edge of the bias tape over the sweatshirt edge. Fuse in place.

7. Continue applying bias tape along bottom edge of sweatshirt, mitering at corners and turning the end under to finish at the top edge of the opposite slit. Topstitch along both edges of the bias tape. Repeat for the back of the shirt. Apply bias tape to edges of sleeves in the same manner.

8. Measure distance from neckline to hem down center of left front. Cut a 4-inch-wide strip of interfacing this length. Fuse to inside of sweatshirt down center of left front (Figure 3). Turn shirt right side out. Mark two parallel lines 1¼ inches apart centered over interfaced area and parallel to sides of sweatshirt.

Figure 3

9. Beginning at the edge of the neckline bias binding, mark grommet placements, spacing 1½ inches apart on the longest line. Center a grommet over each mark and follow manufacturer's instructions to apply using the grommet pliers. Repeat for remaining line, alternating placement with the first row.

10. Interface the inside of each sleeve just above bias tape with a 1½-inch-wide strip of interfacing. Apply seven grommets evenly spaced around each sleeve.

11. Weave lengths of ribbon through grommets, using permanent fabric adhesive to glue ends in place on the inside of the sweatshirt. ❖

Sources: Sweatshirt from Fabric Café; grommets and grommet pliers from Prym Consumer USA Inc.; bias tape from Wrights; Steam-A-Seam2 double-stick fusible web tape from The Warm Company; Fabri-Tac permanent fabric adhesive from Beacon Adhesives.

Divine Diva & Wine

BY PHYLLIS DOBBS

Make a pretty tank top and wine totes with this fanciful design.

FINISHED SIZE
Tank Top: Your size
Tote: Approximately 15 inches long

MATERIALS
- Pink sweatshirt with set-in sleeves
- Cotton print fabric:
    ⅛ yard each aqua and green for tank top
    2 scraps pink and 1 scrap coordinating blue
        for appliquéd tote
- 1½ yards beaded fringe
- 9 (6mm) aqua faceted beads
- 22–24 assorted pink beads
- Metallic ribbon:
    ⅛-inch-wide green
    ⅛-inch wide aqua
- ⅜-inch-wide twill-tape trim:
    1 yard lime green
    ⅔ yard hot pink
- Green embroidery floss
- Fusible web
- Basic sewing supplies and equipment

TANK TOP

DESIGN & ASSEMBLY
Note: *Use ¼-inch seam allowance unless
otherwise stated.*

1. Select, prewash and press sweatshirt as
suggested in General Instructions on page 4.

2. Refer to Cutting Instructions (page 5) to
remove ribbing from sweatshirt neck and bottom
edges. Cut off sleeves. **Note:** *Set sleeves aside
for making totes.*

3. Try on tank top. Pin to mark center front to
determine depth of neckline (approximately
5½ inches from shoulder seam). Pin to mark
hemline at the waist, adding ½ inch for the hem.
Mark armhole opening so the shoulder seam is
2 inches wide. Place tank top on work surface.

4. Referring to Figure 1, draw neckline on one
side of tank top front from top shoulder seam
to center front. Cut on this line. Fold tank top
over and use first half as a pattern to make an
identical cut on the second side. Draw and cut
the back neckline the same way 3 inches below
the shoulder seams. Trim armhole opening.
Try on tank top again. If armhole opening
does not lie flat, pin a 2-inch dart on one side.
Remove tank top.

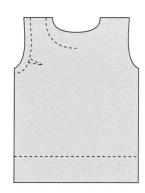

Figure 1

5. Pin a dart in same location for opposite arm
opening. Sew darts, sewing across ends to
reinforce seams.

6. For pockets, cut two 3½ x 3¼-inch rectangles
from aqua fabric and two 3½ x 5-inch rectangles
from green fabric.

7. With right sides together, sew each pair of pocket rectangles together around all four sides, leaving an opening for turning on one 3½-inch edge. Trim corners and turn right side out. Press. Using the photo as a guide, pin pockets to tank top with openings at bottoms. Topstitch around side and bottom edges.

8. Turn up bottom hem ½ inch and press. Pin beaded fringe around bottom, placing fringe band above the fold. Hem, sew ¼ inch from bottom edge, securing hem and beaded fringe. Stitch again ⅜ inch above bottom stitch line.

9. Blanket-stitch around edges of neckline and armhole edges using 3 strands of green embroidery floss. Sew a pink bead at the end of every other blanket stitch around the front of the neckline.

TOTES

CUTTING

1. Cut wristband off sleeve (see Cutting Instructions, page 5). Lay sleeve flat, wrong side out.

2. Draw a straight line from the seam at the narrow end of the sleeve to the opposite end and cut on this line (Figure 2).

3. Cut sleeve ends even. Cut length of sleeve to 16 inches. Open sleeve and place right side up.

EMBROIDERY DESIGN

1. Transfer flower template (page 47) onto center front of sleeve.

Figure 2

2. Using chain stitch, embroider stem and leaves with ¹⁄₁₆-inch-wide green metallic ribbon and the flower with aqua ⅛-inch-wide metallic ribbon. Add a straight stitch on each leaf with green ribbon and at each flower petal tip with aqua ribbon.

3. Referring to photo for placement, sew on aqua beads.

4. Cut a length of lime green twill-tape trim the width of the sleeve when opened flat. Fuse across the sleeve ¼ inch below the flower stem.

APPLIQUÉ DESIGN

Note: *Refer to Appliqué Techniques on page 7.*

1. Using heart template (page 47), apply fusible web to scrap of pink fabric and cut out.

2. Cut three 2¼ x 2¼-inch squares each from the second pink and the blue fabric scraps. Sew together end to end, alternating colors. Press and trim side edges even.

3. Cut strip in half lengthwise to make two identical strips (Figure 3). Apply fusible web to wrong sides of strips.

Figure 3

4. Fuse one strip across opened sleeve 2½ inches from bottom. Fuse second strip 4 inches above first strip. Fuse heart on front of bag, centered between strips. Satin-stitch around edges of appliqués.

ASSEMBLY

1. Fold tote lengthwise, right sides together. Pin side and bottom edges.

2. Fold 24 inches of twill-tape trim in half (lime green for the embroidered tote and hot pink for the appliquéd tote). For ties, insert folded end between side seam 4½ inches from top. Sew seams, catching folded edge of twill-tape trim in stitching.

3. Fold under and stitch a ½-inch hem at top. Turn bag right side out. Knot ends of ties. ❖

Sources: Beaded fringe and aqua beads from Expo International; metallic ribbon from Krienik; Steam-A-Seam2 fusible web from The Warm Company.

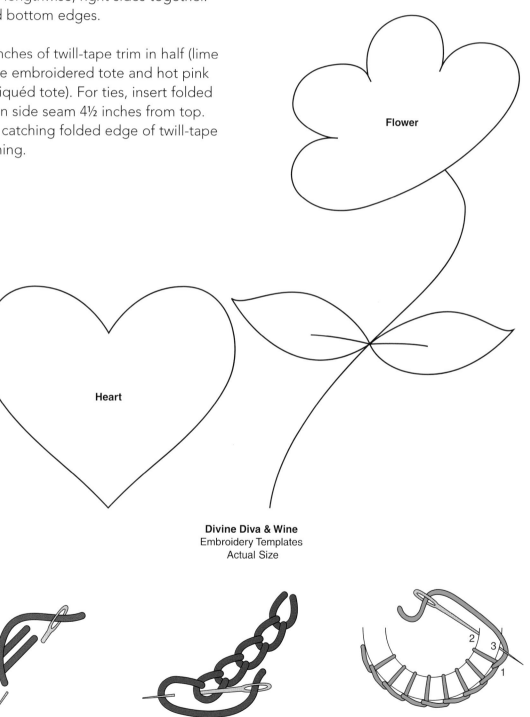

Flower

Heart

Divine Diva & Wine
Embroidery Templates
Actual Size

Straight Stitch

Chain Stitch

Buttonhole Stitch

See, Shop, Sew

BEACON ADHESIVES INC.
(914) 699-3405
www.beaconcreates.com

THE BUTTON EMPORIUM
& RIBBONRY
(503) 228-6372
www.buttonemporium.com

CLOVER NEEDLECRAFT INC.
(800) 233-1703
www.clover-usa.com

CLOTILDE
(800) 772-2891
www.clotilde.com

COATS & CLARK
(800) 648-1479
www.coatsandclark.com

CROWN MOUNTAIN FARMS
(360) 894-1738
www.crownmountainfarms.com

DECOART
(800) 367-3047
www.decoart.com

DHARMA TRADING CO.
(800) 542-5227
www.dharmatrading.com

EXPO INTERNATIONAL
(800) 542-4367
www.expointl.com

FABRIC CAFÉ
(866) 855-0998
www.fabriccafe.com

HOFFMAN CALIFORNIA FABRICS
(800) 547-0100
www.hoffmanfabrics.com

KREINIK
(800) 537-2166
www.kreinik.com

LONDA'S CREATIVE THREADS
(217) 398-5166
www.londas-sewing.com

PELLON CONSUMER PRODUCTS
(800) 223-5275
www.pellonideas.com

PRYM CONSUMER USA INC.
www.prymdritz.com

THE WARM COMPANY
(425) 248-2424
www.warmcompany.com

THE WEAVERS LOFT
(812) 576-3904
www.weaversloft.com

WOODLAND WOOLWORKS
(800) 547-3725
www.woolworks.com

WRIGHTS
(800) 545-5740
www.wrights.com

Designers

JANIS BULLIS
Two-Sided Sweatshirt, page 32

DIANE BUNKER
Twisted-Vine Hoodie, page 26

PHYLLIS DOBBS
Divine Diva & Wine, page 44

ELIZABETH HILL FOR COATS & CLARK
Bolero Vest, page 13

LAURA KEITH
Felted Vest, page 22

JANICE LOEWENTHAL
Sophisticated Swirls, page 38

LORINE MASON
Black & White, page 16

LONDA ROHLFING FOR LONDA'S
CREATIVE THREADS
Fuchsia Fun Jacket, page 8

MISSY SHEPLER
Tailored Tapestry, page 19
Swing on By, page 34

SHEILA ZENT
Coco & Camelot, page 29

CAROL ZENTGRAF
Grommet Accents, page 41

Basic Sewing Supplies & Equipment

- Ballpoint (stretch) sewing machine needles
- Bias tape makers
- Fray Block or seam sealant
- Hand-sewing needles in various sizes and thimble
- Iron glide
- Knit or tricot fusible interfacing
- Marking pens (either air- or water-soluble), tailor's chalk or Chaco liners

- Measuring tools
- Pattern tracing paper or cloth
- Point turners
- Pressing equipment, including ironing board and iron; press cloths
- Pressing tools such as sleeve rolls and June Tailor boards
- Rotary cutter(s), mats and straightedges

- Scissors of various sizes, including pinking shears
- Seam ripper
- Serger, if desired
- Sewing machine and matching thread
- Spray adhesive (temporary)
- Straight pins and pincushion
- Teflon appliqué press cloth
- Wash-A-Way thread
- Wash-A-Way Wonder tape